The 50 More Excel Functions Quiz Book

M.L. HUMPHREY

TITLES BY M.L. HUMPHREY

EXCEL ESSENTIALS
Excel for Beginners
Intermediate Excel
50 Useful Excel Functions
50 More Excel Functions

EXCEL ESSENTIALS QUIZ BOOKS
The Excel for Beginners Quiz Book
The Intermediate Excel Quiz Book
The 50 Useful Excel Functions Quiz Book
The 50 More Excel Functions Quiz Book

DATA PRINCIPLES
Data Principles for Beginners

EASY EXCEL ESSENTIALS
Pivot Tables
Conditional Formatting
Charts
The IF Functions
Formatting
Printing

WORD ESSENTIALS
Word for Beginners
Intermediate Word

MAIL MERGE
Mail Merge for Beginners

POWERPOINT ESSENTIALS
PowerPoint for Beginners

BUDGETING FOR BEGINNERS
Budgeting for Beginners
Excel for Budgeting

.

CONTENTS

INTRODUCTION

This is a companion book written to complement *50 More Excel Functions* by M.L. Humphrey and is geared towards those who are already familiar with the functions covered in that book who now want to test their knowledge through quizzes or to those who learn better from a question and answer format.

The quizzes in this book are in the same order as in *50 More Excel Functions* but are sometimes grouped by related functions. So one quiz might cover, for example, functions related to basic math.

The first section of the book just has the questions, the next section of the book has the questions as well as the answers. There is also a bonus section that contains five exercises where you can test your knowledge of the various functions by applying them to specific real-life scenarios.

I encourage you to try to do each exercise first without looking at the solutions, since in the real world you'll be faced with a problem that needs solved and no one will be there to tell you which functions to use. However, I would also encourage you to have Excel open as you work each exercise so you can use the help functions within Excel to find the functions you need. Don't feel like you need to memorize every function in Excel in order to use it effectively. You just need to know what's possible and then what keywords or phrasing to use to help you find the right function.

Finally, both *50 Useful Excel Functions* and *50 More Excel Functions* cover the same basic information about how formulas and functions work so there is overlap in the quizzes for each book. If you've already read *The 50 Useful Excel Functions Quiz Book*, then you can skip those quizzes because they're identical to the ones contained in that book.

Alright, then. Let's start with the first quiz.

QUIZZES

HOW FORMULAS AND
FUNCTIONS WORK QUIZ

1. If you're writing a basic formula in Excel, what symbols can you use to indicate this to Excel?

2. If you're starting a formula using a function in Excel, which symbol do you need to use to indicate this to Excel?

3. If you enter a formula in Excel and then hit enter, what are you going to see in that cell in your worksheet?

4. If you want to see the actual formula that's in a cell, how can you do that?

5. What is the difference between a formula and a function?

6. What are the symbols you can use for adding, subtracting, multiplying, or dividing in Excel?

7. What do the following formulas do?

    A. =3+2

    B. =3-2

    C. =3*2

    D. =3/2

    E. =4+(3*2)

    F. =4+3*2

8. What do the following formulas do?

    A. =A1+C1

    B. =A1-C1

    C. =A1*C1

    D. =A1/C1

    E. =E1+(A1*C1)

    F. =E1+A1*C1

9. What do examples E and F of the last two questions above demonstrate?

10. What's a best practice when building a really complex formula in Excel?

11. How do you write a function in Excel when it's at the beginning of a formula?

12. Can you use more than once function within a single cell in Excel?

13. What happens if you give the wrong cell range for your function?

WHERE TO FIND FUNCTIONS QUIZ

1. In newer versions of Excel where can you go to look for a function to perform a specific task?

2. What are the categories of functions available in Excel?

3. If you bring up the Insert Function dialogue box and are looking to perform a specific task with a function, where can you search for that?

4. What happens when you click on a function name under Select a Function in the Insert Function dialogue box?

5. If that's not enough information, what can you do?

6. What happens when you select a function from the Insert Function dialogue box?

7. If you already know the function you want to use, but aren't sure of the inputs or the order they need to be entered in, what can you do within your Excel worksheet?

8. If you click on the function name after you've typed, =FUNCTION_NAME(what will you get?

9. What if you still can't figure out what function to use to do what you want to do or don't even know if a function exists for what you're looking to do?

10. What can you do if you're using a version of Excel that's prior to Excel 2007 and so don't have a Formulas tab to go to but want to bring up the Insert Function dialogue box?

FORMULA AND FUNCTION BEST PRACTICES QUIZ

1. Name four best practices when working with formulas or functions.

2. Explain what it means to make your assumptions visible.

3. Explain what it means to use paste special-values when you're done with your calculations and when you should not do this.

4. How can you paste special-values to replace a formula with just the result of the formula?

5. Explain why you should store your raw data in one location and work on a copy of that data instead.

6. What's another best practice when doing a lot of complex work with a dataset that requires multiple steps and manipulations?

7. Why should you test your formulas before applying them to a large data set?

8. Why can't you just accept the results Excel gives you? Why should you always "gut check" those results?

COPYING FORMULAS QUIZ

1. What happens when you copy a formula from one cell to another?

2. If you write a formula and you want to fix the reference to a specific cell so that even if the formula is copied elsewhere it continues to reference that cell, how can you do this?

3. What if you just want to lock the row reference but not the entire cell reference?

4. What if you just want to lock the column reference but not the entire cell reference?

5. If you just want to move a formula to a new location without it changing, what's the best way to do that?

THE IFNA AND
IFERROR QUIZ

1. What function can you use to suppress an #N/A! result in a formula?

2. Apply that function to the following formula: =VLOOKUP(D:D,'Advertising Spend By Series'!E:F,2, FALSE) so that a value of 0 is returned instead of the #N/A! error message.

3. Now apply the function to the following formula: =VLOOKUP(D:D,'Advertising Spend By Series'!E:F,2, FALSE)so that a value of "No Match" is returned instead of the #N/A! error message.

4. And also apply the function to the following formula: =VLOOKUP(D:D,'Advertising Spend By Series'!E:F,2, FALSE) so that a blank value is returned instead of the #N/A! error message.

5. What function can you use to suppress all error messages instead of just #N/A!?

6. Apply that function to a situation where you are dividing the value in Cell A1 by the value in Cell B1 and you want to return a blank result instead of an error message.

7. Now apply that function to a situation where you are dividing the value in Cell A1 by the value in Cell B1 and you want to return a value of "Error" instead of a specific error message.

8. What is the danger in using IFNA or IFERROR?

9. What is one way of addressing this issue?

THE NOT
FUNCTION QUIZ

1. What functions is the NOT function related to?

2. Why do I encourage you to find a way to use a function other than the NOT function to build a formula?

3. What result will you get if you use =NOT(FALSE)?

4. What result will you get if you use =NOT(TRUE)?

5. How could you use the NOT function?

6. Take the formula =NOT(B5<12). What value will it return if the value in Cell B5 is 2? What about if it's 14?

7. How could you evaluate that condition (whether B5 is less than 12 or equal to or greater than 12) with an IF function and get the same result as using the NOT function above?

THE HLOOKUP
FUNCTION QUIZ

1. What function is the HLOOKUP function related to?

2. What does HLOOKUP do?

3. What will this formula do:
     =HLOOKUP("April",B1:M12,4,FALSE)

4. What can you look up using HLOOKUP?

5. If you look up a text string, what do you need to be sure to do?

6. What are wildcards and how can you use them when looking up text?

7. In the table you're going to search using HLOOKUP, where do the values you're searching for need to be?

8. In the table you're going to search using HLOOKUP, where do the values you want to return need to be?

9. What is the difference between using FALSE and TRUE as the final input to the HLOOKUP function?

10. What is the risk to using TRUE as the third input to the HLOOKUP function?

11. Can you sort the values in a row in ascending order?

12. When you tell Excel which row to pull your result from using HLOOKUP, what number do you need to provide? Is it the Row number in the worksheet or something else?

13. If you provide a row value of 1 in the HLOOKUP function what will that return?

14. If you ask HLOOKUP to find an exact match and there isn't one, what value will Excel return?

15. What could potentially result in an incorrect error message when using HLOOKUP?

THE TRANSPOSE
FUNCTION QUIZ

1. What does the TRANSPOSE function do?

2. Does TRANSPOSE work on a table of values that covers multiple rows and/or columns?

3. What do you have to do special because TRANSPOSE is an array formula?

4. If you want to take the values in Cells C1 through C5 and place them in Cells E8 through I8, how would you do that?

5. If all you want to do is change the orientation of your data, what is a better option?

6. What benefit does the TRANSPOSE function give over doing that?

THE INDEX
FUNCTION QUIZ

1. What are the two tasks that the INDEX function can perform?

2. What is the following formula supposed to do: =INDEX(A2:E7,3,4)

3. Does the INDEX function require you to include a header row or row labels in the specified cell range?

4. How do you determine the row number value to use in the INDEX function?

5. How do you determine the column number value to use in the INDEX function?

6. Can you use the INDEX function with more than one table of data? How?

7. What happens if you use the fourth variable in the INDEX function without providing multiple table range values in the first variable?

8. If you want to use the INDEX function to pull an entire column or row of data, what do you need to do?

9. Can you easily copy and paste an array formula?

10. Once you've extracted values from a table using the INDEX function are the results fixed values?

THE MATCH
FUNCTION QUIZ

1. What does the MATCH function do?

2. If the MATCH function returns a value of 2 for the following formula, what does that mean:
$$=MATCH(\$A12,\$A\$2:\$A\$7,0)$$

3. What is the value in using the MATCH function?

4. What kinds of values can MATCH look for?

5. What are the three match types that you can use with MATCH?

6. If you're not looking for an exact match what do you need to do first? And how will your choice of match type impact this?

7. What is the default match type used by MATCH? Why is this a problem?

8. Is the value returned by MATCH the row number or the column number in the worksheet or something else?

TEXT FUNCTIONS
QUIZ

1. What does the LEN function do?

2. What does the SEARCH function do?

3. What does the FIND function do?

4. So what is the difference between SEARCH and FIND?

5. If you're working in a language such as Japanese, Chinese, or Korean that uses bytes instead of characters what functions should you use instead of LEN, SEARCH, and FIND?

6. What does the EXACT function do?

7. Is EXACT case-sensitive?

8. What result would LEN return for =LEN("This one")? Why?

9. Can you use LEN with a cell reference, so for example, =LEN(D10)?

10. How does LEN handle a formula in a cell?

11. What is the following formula doing:
$$=LEFT(A1,LEN(A1)-LEN(" units"))?$$

12. How could you accomplish the same task using the SEARCH function? Explain why this works.

13. Do you have to start at the beginning of a text string if using the SEARCH or FIND functions?

14. If you do use the third input in the SEARCH or FIND function, what do you need to keep in mind about the value that's returned?

15. What will your result be if the value you search for using SEARCH or FIND isn't in that text string?

16. What will your result be if the start position you provide is a negative number or a larger number than the length of the text string in SEARCH or FIND?

17. What values will =SEARCH("coz*","teacozy") and =FIND("coz*","teacozy") return? Why?

18. What values will =SEARCH("t","Teapot") and =FIND("t","Teapot") return? Why?

19. Does EXACT look for differences in formatting between two entries?

20. If you wanted to compare the values in Cells A1 and D2, how would you write that using the EXACT function? What value would you expect if the two values were equal?

What would you expect if they were not?

21. If you use EXACT with two cells that use different formulas but return the same numeric value, what will the result be?

THE CONVERT FUNCTION
QUIZ

1. What does the CONVERT function do?

2. Name three types of conversions CONVERT can do:

3. What happens if you use units from two different categories in the same CONVERT function?

4. Are the units used in the CONVERT function case-sensitive?

5. Write the formula for converting 57 degrees Fahrenheit to Celsius:

6. Write the formula for determining how many days there are in five years using the CONVERT function:

7. Give a likely explanation for why the value returned in the last example is a decimal:

8. Write the formula for converting 60 miles to kilometers.

NUMERIC FUNCTIONS QUIZ

1. What function would you use to take the absolute value of a number?

2. Write the function for the absolute value of -3:

3. What does the MOD function do?

4. What does the QUOTIENT function do?

5. Can you use the MOD and QUOTIENT functions to take a decimal number, such as 12.345 and separate the integer portion from the decimal portion? If so, how?

6. What is another function that allows you to extract just the integer portion of a number?

7. Apply this function to 12.345 to get 12:

8. What is the difference between truncating a number and rounding a number?

9. How would you truncate 12,543 to the nearest 1000s?

10. Is this the same value you'd get if you rounded to the nearest 1000s?

11. How does the INT function differ from the ROUND and TRUNC functions?

12. How would you use the TRUNC function (and perhaps another function) to separate the number -12.345 into its integer and decimal components?

POWERS AND SQUARE
ROOTS QUIZ

1. What does it mean to raise a number to a power?

2. What function can be used to do this?

3. Is there a way to do this with notation instead? How?

4. Show how to take 5 to the power of 4 using both the function and the notation method.

5. Can you use both of these methods to take a root power, such as the square root of a number? If so, write how to take the square root of 9.

6. Is there a function that will specifically let you take the square root of a number? What is it? Apply it to 9.

7. What is the function that will let you return the value of Pi to fifteen digits?

8. How would you write that?

9. How would you calculate the area of a circle (which is Pi times the square of the radius) using the above functions where the radius is 3?

10. What does the function SQRTPI give you?

11. If you wanted the square root of Pi itself, how could you get that value?

LOGARITHMS QUIZ

1. What formula would you use to obtain the value of e?

2. What does the function used in the prior question do?

3. What is =LOG(100) asking?

4. Write a formula that uses the LOG function to determine what power you'd have to take the number 2 to get a result of 24:

5. Write a formula that uses the LOG function to determine what power you'd have to take e to to get a result of 24:

6. Write a formula that uses the LN function to make the same determination:

7. What does the LN function do?

8. What does the LOG function do?

9. Which of the two is more flexible?

10. What does the LOG10 function do?

11. Should you use it?

FACTORIALS AND COMBINATIONS QUIZ

1. What is the difference between permutations and combinations?

2. What does a factorial do?

3. What function in Excel will do this calculation for you?

4. What formula would you write to determine the number of possible permutations for a group of ten people?

5. What happens with the FACT function if you input a decimal value, for example =FACT(3.95)?

6. What value will Excel return if you ask for the factorial of zero?

7. What happens if you ask for the factorial of a negative number?

8. If you had a group of ten individuals and wanted to give out first, second, and third place medals, how would you use the FACT function to calculate the number of possible three-person outcomes?

9. What if you instead wanted to calculate the number of three-person teams that could be built out of a population of nine people. What function would you use?

10. What does this function do?

11. How would you use it to calculate the number of two-person teams possible in a group of four individuals?

12. What function would you use if you want to know the number of possible combinations where each possibility can be chosen multiple times? (In other words, you can have 22 as an outcome.)

13. So if you had a raffle drawing and there were ten people participating, each with one ticket and where each ticket was put back into the draw each time, and you wanted to know the odds of one person winning all three draws how would you do that calculation?

PRESENT AND FUTURE VALUES QUIZ

1. If you want to know the current value of a series of identical payments that you'll receive on an annual basis in the future, what function can you use to calculate that?

2. What are the inputs to this function?

3. What does the NPV function do?

4. What is the advantage of the NPV function over the PV function?

5. What limitation do both PV and NPV share?

6. If I have a range of values in Cells B2 through B8 that represent annual payments I'm going to receive starting one year from now and want to calculate the net present value of those amounts using a ten percent annual interest rate, how would I write that:

7. What if I'm going to receive $1,000 each year for the next five years and the annual interest rate is 10%. What formula would you write to calculate the current value of those future payments?

8. What does the FORECAST function do?

9. Why is it important to remember that it only works with a linear trend?

10. Because of this, what should you do before using the FORECAST function?

11. What are the order of the inputs to the FORECAST function?

12. Can you use FORECAST to predict a value prior to your data range? In other words, what y would be at a smaller value of x than is shown in your data table?

THE FREQUENCY FUNCTION QUIZ

1. What does the FREQUENCY function do?

2. What must you have in order to use the FREQUENCY function?

3. What does it mean that FREQUENCY is an array function?

4. What are the inputs to the FREQUENCY function?

5. How is a bins array entry structured? And how is it used by Excel?

6. What is an easy way to get a list of bin array values that correspond to all potential values in your data set?

7. If the range of values you want to evaluate are in Column C and your bins values are in Cells D2 through D6, how would you write the formula to calculate your frequencies for each of those bin values?

THE HOW EXCEL HANDLES
DATES QUIZ

1. By default what does the number 1 represent with respect to a date in Excel?

2. Can Excel handle dates prior to 1900?

3. Can you use addition and subtraction with dates in Excel? Why or why not?

4. What is a serial_number with respect to date functions in Excel?

5. How does Excel handle dates differently on the Mac operating system? What does this mean for someone working between a PC and a Mac using Excel?

6. How does Excel account for this?

7. If you enter a two-digit year, for example '29, how will Excel treat that in terms of the century it applies?

DATE FUNCTIONS
QUIZ

1. What does the DATE function do?

2. What happens if you use the DATE function with a date prior to January 1, 1900, so for example if you use =DATE(1880,1,1)?

3. Can you use a value for the month portion of the DATE function that is greater than 12? What about less than 1?

4. What about days of the month? Can you have a number greater than 31 or a negative number?

5. Write a formula that takes a date stored in Cell B2 and adds four months to it.

6. What does the YEAR function do?

7. How would you use YEAR to extract the year portion of the date March 1, 2010?

8. What happens if you fail to use quotation marks around a date used in a YEAR function?

9. What does the MONTH function do?

10. What result will you get from =MONTH("April, 1, 1952")?

11. What does the DAY function do?

12. What does the HOUR function do?

13. What will =HOUR(NOW()) give you?

14. Since Excel treats dates as numbers, what is the value of an hour under Excel's system?

15. Will you get a result with =HOUR(.166667)?

16. How does the MINUTE function work?

17. Since Excel treats dates as numbers, what is the value of a minute under Excel's system?

18. What does the SECOND function do?

19. What result will you get from
                    =SECOND("12:32:21")?

20. Since Excel treats dates as numbers, what is the value of a second under Excel's system?

21. If you enter a date without entering a specific time of day and then use the HOUR, MINUTE, or SECOND function on that date, what value will Excel give you?

22. What does the WEEKDAY function do?

23. What is the default setting for the WEEKDAY function in terms of numbering the days of the week?

24. If August 13, 2019 is a Tuesday and I use =WEEKDAY("August 13, 2019") what value will I get back?

25. What portion of the WEEKDAY function should you change if you want the numbers returned to map to different days of the week? How would you change the above formula so that Monday is treated as a 1 and Tuesday returns a value of 2 instead?

26. What does the following formula do:
        =IF(WEEKDAY(A1,2)>5,12.95,9.95)

27. What does the WEEKNUM function do?

28. How does Excel define a week for purposes of the WEEKNUM function?

29. How do you get Excel to define a week in accordance with ISO standards when using the WEEKNUM function? And how does it work?

30. What is another function you can use to get Excel to apply the ISO standard when determining the week number? And when did it become available?

DATE CALCULATION FUNCTIONS IN EXCEL QUIZ

1. What does the DAYS function do?

2. Do you need the DAYS function to do this?

3. What does the DAYS360 function do?

4. Are there different methods with DAYS360 for handling the last day of the month when it's either in February or in a month with 31 days?

5. What does the EDATE function do?

6. What is another way to get this same result?

7. If I use =EDATE("March 1, 2019",4) what result will that give me?

8. How does EDATE handle partial month values, such as =EDATE("March 1, 2019",4.9)?

9. What does the EOMONTH function do?

10. What do you need to do with the result of an EDATE or EOMONTH formula?

WORKDAYS AND NETWORKDAYS QUIZ

1. What does the NETWORKDAYS function do?

2. How is this different from just using the DAYS function?

3. How can you incorporate holidays into the NETWORKDAYS function?

4. What if you don't want NETWORKDAYS to include the start date and the end date in the calculation?

5. Using NETWORKDAYS write a formula calculating the number of workdays between August 28, 2019 and September 4, 2019 where September 2, 2019 is a holiday and you don't want to count the first or the last day in the count:

6. What function would you use to calculate workdays if your weekend days are not Saturday and Sunday?

7. With which version of Excel did this function become available?

8. Explain what the weekend input to the NETWORKDAYS.INTL function does:

9. Are NETWORKDAYS and NETWORKDAYS.INTL directly interchangeable? Can you just change one to the other and have it work?

10. What does the WORKDAY function do?

11. Does WORKDAY include the start date in its count like NETWORKDAYS does?

12. What does the WORKDAY.INTL function do?

13. Let's say that your team is working six-day weeks and that they're allowed to have Wednesdays off. It's currently August 23, 2019 and your team says they need twelve more days to finish the project. There is a holiday on September 2, 2019. When will they complete the project?

14. What if they tell you this on the morning of the 23rd and you know that they'll be working all day so it will count towards their timeline. Will this impact the completion date?

15. Can you create a custom set of off days using the WORKDAY.INTL function? How?

COMBINING FUNCTIONS QUIZ

1. Is it possible to write a formula that uses more than one function?

2. How would you write a formula that returns a value of TRUE if the value in Cell A1 is greater than 10 or the value in Cell B1 is greater than 10 and a value of FALSE otherwise?

3. What do you need to be careful about when combining functions together in one formula?

4. Do you need to use an equals sign in front of each function name when you combine functions in a single formula?

5. What should you explore further if you're running into file size issues because of repeat calculations in your Excel worksheet?

WHEN THINGS GO
WRONG QUIZ

1. Name five different error messages you might see.

2. What does #REF! generally indicate?

3. How can you see where the cell that was deleted was located in your formula?

4. What does a #VALUE! message indicate?

5. What does a #DIV/0! message indicate?

6. If the #DIV/0! message is legitimate because nothing has been entered yet, what's a quick way to suppress it?

7. What does a #N/A error message generally mean?

8. What can you check for if this happens and you don't think it should have?

9. What does the IFERROR function do? What do you need to be careful with if you use it?

10. What does the #NUM! error message generally indicate?

11. What is a circular reference?

12. If you don't think you have a circular reference but Excel tells you you do, what should you check for?

13. If you're trying to figure out what cells are feeding the value in a cell where can you go to do that?

14. If Excel tells you you have too few arguments, what should you check for?

15. What can you do with a formula that just isn't working the way it should be?

CELL NOTATION QUIZ

1. What is Cell A1 referencing?

2. Name two ways you can reference more than one cell in a function.

3. Can you reference a cell in another worksheet?

4. Can you reference a cell in another workbook?

5. What's an easy way to reference a cell in another worksheet or workbook?

QUIZ ANSWERS

HOW FORMULAS AND FUNCTIONS WORK QUIZ ANSWERS

1. If you're writing a basic formula in Excel, what symbols can you use to indicate this to Excel?

You can use a plus sign (+), a minus sign (-), or an equals sign (=).

2. If you're starting a formula using a function in Excel, which symbol do you need to use to indicate this to Excel?

The equals sign (=).

3. If you enter a formula in Excel and then hit enter, what are you going to see in that cell in your worksheet?

The result. So, for example, if you type =2+2 into a cell and hit enter you will see 4, the result of adding two plus two, in the cell where you entered the formula.

4. If you want to see the actual formula that's in a cell, how can you do that?

Click on the cell and look in the formula bar or double-click on the cell to see the formula in the cell itself.

5. What is the difference between a formula and a function?

A function lets you perform a specified task. It's like a programmed shortcut. That task can be mathematical (like SUM) or it can be related to text (like CONCATENATE), dates, or logic. A formula is a way of performing a calculation using Excel and it can not only involve functions but also just basic math notation.

6. What are the symbols you can use for adding, subtracting, multiplying, or dividing in Excel?

To add you can use the plus sign (+). To subtract you can use the minus sign (-). To multiply you can use the asterisk (*). And to divide you can use the forward slash (/).

7. What do the following formulas do?

A. =3+2

Adds 3 to 2

B. =3-2

Subtracts 2 from 3

C. =3*2

Multiplies 3 by 2

D. =3/2

Divides 3 by 2

E. =4+(3*2)

Multiplies 3 by 2 and then adds the result to 4

F. =4+3*2

Adds 4 to 3 and then multiplies the result by 2

8. What do the following formulas do?
A. =A1+C1

Adds the value in A1 to the value in C1

B. =A1-C1
Subtracts the value in C1 from the value in A1

C. =A1*C1
Multiplies the value in A1 by the value in C1

D. =A1/C1
Divides the value in A1 by the value in C1

E. =E1+(A1*C1)
Multiplies the value in A1 by the value in C1 and then adds the result to the value in E1

F. =E1+A1*C1
Adds the value in E1 to the value in A1 and then multiplies the result by the value in C1

9. What do examples E and F from the last two questions above demonstrate?

How important it is when writing a complex formula that you place your parens in the right place, because that will determine the order in which Excel performs its calculations and will impact your answer.

10. What's a best practice when building a really complex formula in Excel?

Build it in pieces and test that each piece is calculating correctly before combining all of the pieces together.

11. How do you write a function in Excel when it's at the beginning of a formula?

=FUNCTION_NAME(

You start with an equals sign, follow that with the function name, and then immediately follow that with an opening paren.

12. Can you use more than once function within a single cell in Excel?

Yes.

13. What happens if you give the wrong cell range for your function?

Garbage in, garbage out. It won't do what you want it to do. For a function to properly work it needs to be the right one and you need to give it the right inputs in the right order.

WHERE TO FIND FUNCTIONS
QUIZ ANSWERS

1. In newer versions of Excel where can you go to look for a function to perform a specific task?

The Formulas tab will show you a Function Library set of dropdowns arranged by type (Financial, Logical, Text, etc.) and you can hold your mouse over each one for a brief description of what it does. But if you don't know the function you want, it's better to go to Insert Function and bring up the Insert Function dialogue box. This will let you search using a few keywords for the function you want.

2. What are the categories of functions available in Excel?

Financial, Logical, Text, Date & Time, Lookup & Reference, Math & Trig, Statistical, Engineering, Cube, Information, Compatibility, Web

3. If you bring up the Insert Function dialogue box and are looking to perform a specific task with a function, where can you search for that?

In the Search For a Function box at the top. Enter a few keywords related to what you want to do and then click on Go. Excel will list functions in the Select a Function box that meet those keywords.

4. What happens when you click on a function name under Select a Function in the Insert Function dialogue box?

Excel will show you a brief description of what the function does as well as a sample of what inputs the function requires to work.

5. If that's not enough information, what can you do?

Click on Help on This Function in the bottom left corner.

6. What happens when you select a function from the Insert Function dialogue box?

It brings up the Function Arguments box which will show you the description for the function, a sample output for the function based upon the choices you make, and input boxes for you to add the information required for the function.

7. If you already know the function you want to use, but aren't sure of the inputs or the order they need to be entered in, what can you do within your Excel worksheet?

Type =FUNCTION_NAME to see the Excel description of what the function does. Type =FUNCTION_NAME(to see a list of the inputs for the function and the order in which they need to appear.

8. If you click on the function name after you've typed, =FUNCTION_NAME(what will you get?

An Excel Help dialogue box for that function.

9. What if you still can't figure out what function to use to do what you want to do or don't even know if a

function exists for what you're looking to do?

Do an internet search. Chances are someone else at some point wanted to do the exact same thing you do.

10. What can you do if you're using a version of Excel that's prior to Excel 2007 and so don't have a Formulas tab to go to but want to bring up the Insert Function dialogue box?

Type an equals sign into a cell, go to the white dropdown box to the left of the formula bar, click on the dropdown arrow, and choose More Functions from the bottom of the list.

FORMULA AND FUNCTION BEST PRACTICES QUIZ ANSWERS

1. Name four best practices when working with formulas or functions.

Make your assumptions visible, use paste special-values when you're done with your calculations, store your raw data in one location and work on a copy of that data for any calculations or manipulations, test your formulas to make sure they work under all possible circumstances especially threshold cases.

2. Explain what it means to make your assumptions visible.

While it's possible to write a formula that has all of the information written within a cell, it's better to show on your worksheet any inputs into that formula. For example, if I assume that selling my house is going to cost me 3% in realtor fees, it's better to have a field in Excel for realtor fees that I can see at a glance and to reference that cell with my formula than to build that 3% amount into a formula where I'll only see it if I click on that cell. (Especially since that number is very likely wrong.)

3. Explain what it means to use paste special-values when you're done with your calculations and when you should not do this.

Do not do this if you expect to update your information that's feeding the calculation. This should only be done when you are completely finished with your analysis. Because if you do it and then update an input into the formula, the formula no longer exists and your final answer will not update with the new information.

But the reason to do this is the same. If you've finished your calculation using paste special-values will lock in your results so that they can't be impacted by deleting data that was used to make the calculation.

4. How can you paste special-values to replace a formula with just the result of the formula?

Click on the cell with formula and Copy (Ctrl +C is the easiest way to do this), right-click on the same cell, and choose to Paste Special and then the Values option from the dropdown menu. (It's the one with the 123 on the clipboard.)

5. Explain why you should store your raw data in one location and work on a copy of that data instead.

Because some things can't be undone. If you sort only part of your data, for example, and don't realize it until later your entire dataset will be useless. Or if you find and replace the wrong information. Or you remove duplicates from only part of your data. Etc.

6. What's another best practice when doing a lot of complex work with a dataset that requires multiple steps and manipulations?

Save versions of the data as you go after each significant manipulation is completed. This way if you do mess up at some point along the way you can go back to one of those earlier versions rather than having to start over from scratch.

7. Why should you test your formulas before applying them to a large data set?

To make sure they're working properly, especially at the thresholds. So, for example, if you're using an IF function that returns one value when the value in Column A is over 25 and another value when it's under, you should test what happens when the value in Column A is 25. Is that the result you want? If not, you need to edit the formula. And it's easier to catch these things in test scenarios that are designed to test the edges than in a thousand rows of data.

8. Why can't you just accept the results Excel gives you? Why should you always "gut check" those results?

Because Excel just does what you tell it to do and if you tell it to do the wrong thing it's going to do it without question. So you should always be asking yourself, "does this result make sense"? And if it doesn't, you need to look at the numbers and your result to see if there's an error in your formula.

COPYING FORMULAS
QUIZ ANSWERS

1. What happens when you copy a formula from one cell to another?

All cell references in the formula will adjust based upon the number of rows and columns you moved the formula. So if a formula references Cell A1 and you move it over two columns, that reference to Cell A1 will become a reference to Cell C1. And if you move it down two rows, that reference to Cell A1 will become a reference to Cell A3.

2. If you write a formula and you want to fix the reference to a specific cell so that even if the formula is copied elsewhere it continues to reference that cell, how can you do this?

By using $ signs in front of both the column and row reference. So if you use $A$1 in a formula and copy that formula, the formula will continue to reference Cell A1 no matter where you copy it to.

3. What if you just want to lock the row reference but not the entire cell reference?

Then just put a $ sign in front of the row portion of the cell reference. So, for example, A$1.

4. What if you just want to lock the column reference but not the entire cell reference?

Then just put a $ sign in front of the column portion of the cell reference. So, for example, $A1.

5. If you just want to move a formula to a new location without it changing, what's the best way to do that?

Use Cut instead of Copy. That will move the formula without changing the cell references.

THE IFNA AND IFERROR QUIZ ANSWERS

1. What function can you use to suppress an #N/A! result in a formula?

The IFNA function.

2. Apply that function to the following formula: =VLOOKUP(D:D,'Advertising Spend By Series'!E:F, 2,FALSE) so that a value of 0 is returned instead of the #N/A! error message.

=IFNA(VLOOKUP(D:D,'Advertising Spend By Series'!E:F,2,FALSE),0)

3. Now apply the function to the following formula: =VLOOKUP(D:D,'Advertising Spend By Series'!E:F, 2,FALSE)so that a value of "No Match" is returned instead of the #N/A! error message.

=IFNA(VLOOKUP(D:D,'Advertising Spend By Series'!E:F,2,FALSE),"No Match")

4. And also apply the function to the following formula: =VLOOKUP(D:D,'Advertising Spend By

Series'!E:F,2,FALSE) so that a blank value is returned instead of the #N/A! error message.

$$=IFNA(VLOOKUP(D:D,'Advertising\ Spend\ By$$
$$Series'!E:F,2,FALSE),"")$$

5. What function can you use to suppress all error messages instead of just #N/A!?

The IFERROR function.

6. Apply that function to a situation where you are dividing the value in Cell A1 by the value in Cell B1 and you want to return a blank result instead of an error message.

=IFERROR(A1/B1,"")

7. Now apply that function to a situation where you are dividing the value in Cell A1 by the value in Cell B1 and you want to return a value of "Error" instead of a specific error message.

=IFERROR(A1/B1,"Error")

8. What is the danger in using IFNA or IFERROR?

They may suppress a legitimate error message that you need to see. A #N/A! error can indicate that you have, for example, a formatting or spelling error in a list of values. And a #DIV/0! error can indicate you're missing a value you thought you had or that you're using the wrong cell in your equation.

9. What is one way of addressing this issue?

Have the formula return a text value instead of a value of zero or a blank value. This will indicate that an error message was generated by the calculation so that you can properly review it without interfering with any calculations on those cells.

THE NOT FUNCTION QUIZ ANSWERS

1. What functions is the NOT function related to?
The AND and OR functions.

2. Why do I encourage you to find a way to use a function other than the NOT function to build a formula?
Because using a negative to build a formula is counter to how most people think.

3. What result will you get if you use =NOT(FALSE)?
TRUE

4. What result will you get if you use =NOT(TRUE)?
FALSE

5. How could you use the NOT function?
To evaluate whether a criteria was met in a more complex formula.

6. Take the formula =NOT(B5<12). What value will it return if the value in Cell B5 is 2? What about if it's 14?
FALSE. TRUE.

7. How could you evaluate that condition (whether B5 is less than 12 or equal to or greater than 12) with an IF function and get the same result as using the NOT function above?

=IF(B5>12,TRUE) or =IF(B5>12,TRUE,FALSE)

THE HLOOKUP FUNCTION QUIZ
ANSWERS

1. What function is the HLOOKUP function related to?

The VLOOKUP function.

2. What does HLOOKUP do?

It scans across a row of data to match a value you specify and then pulls a result from another row in the same column where that match was made. For example, you could scan for a month in a table with month values across the top and then pull the specific result for a vendor if vendor results were listed in rows below each month.

3. What will this formula do:
=HLOOKUP("April",B1:M12,4,FALSE)

It will look for a cell with the value "April" in row one of the data set contained in Cells B1 through M12 and then will go to the fourth row of that column and pull the value in the corresponding cell. In this case, a value will only be returned if there is an exact match to "April".

4. What can you look up using HLOOKUP?

A numeric value, a text string, or a cell reference.

5. If you look up a text string, what do you need to be sure to do?

Put quotation marks around the text string you want to look up.

6. What are wildcards and how can you use them when looking up text?

A wildcard, like * or ?, allows you to look up text without being exact about what text you're looking up. For example, "*April" would look up any text string that has April at the very end no matter how long the text string. So it would include "I like the month of April" as a valid match. On the other hand, "?April" will look for any text string that has one character before April. So "1April" would be a valid match but "20th April" would not.

7. In the table you're going to search using HLOOKUP, where do the values you're searching for need to be?

The first row of the range specified in the function.

8. In the table you're going to search using HLOOKUP, where do the values you want to return need to be?

In the lookup row or in the rows below the lookup row.

9. What is the difference between using FALSE and TRUE as the final input to the HLOOKUP function?

Using FALSE means that only an exact match will return a value. Using TRUE will return an approximate value.

10. What is the risk to using TRUE as the third input to the HLOOKUP function?

If your data isn't sorted in ascending order before you use the function, the value returned may not be the closest value.

11. Can you sort the values in a row in ascending order?

Yes. It's an option under the Sort function in Excel. Choose the Sort Left to Right option.

12. When you tell Excel which row to pull your result from using HLOOKUP, what number do you need to provide? Is it the Row number in the worksheet or something else?

No, it is not the row number in the worksheet. It's the row within the table specified in the HLOOKUP function.

13. If you provide a row value of 1 in the HLOOKUP function what will that return?

Either the value you were looking if you were looking for an exact match (FALSE) or the closest value if you were looking for an approximate value (TRUE).

14. If you ask HLOOKUP to find an exact match and there isn't one, what value will Excel return?

#N/A!

15. What could potentially result in an incorrect error message when using HLOOKUP?

A spelling error in the formula, extra spaces in the entries that are being looked at, an incorrect table range, incorrect row references, or a lookup value outside the range in the table.

THE TRANSPOSE FUNCTION QUIZ
ANSWERS

1. What does the TRANSPOSE function do?

It converts a vertical range of cells to a horizontal range or vice versa. In other words, it take a range of values in a row and puts them in a column or takes a range of values in a column and puts them in a row instead.

2. Does TRANSPOSE work on a table of values that covers multiple rows and/or columns?

Yes.

3. What do you have to do special because TRANSPOSE is an array formula?

Two things. You must first select the range of cells where you want your result to go before you start typing your formula in the first cell of the range. And you must also use Ctrl+Shift+Enter when you finish entering the formula (rather than just Enter) for it to work.

4. If you want to take the values in Cells C1 through C5 and place them in Cells E8 through I8, how would you do that?

Highlight Cells E8 through I8. Type in the formula

=TRANSPOSE(C1:C5) in Cell E8 (while keeping the other cells highlighted). Finish with Ctrl+Shift+Enter.

5. If all you want to do is change the orientation of your data, what is a better option?

Use Copy and Paste-Transpose instead.

6. What benefit does the TRANSPOSE function give over doing that?

When you use the TRANSPOSE function the values in your cells are still linked to their original source, so a change in the value in the original location will change the transposed value as well. When you use Copy and Paste-Transpose those pasted values are now separate from the original source values..

THE INDEX FUNCTION QUIZ ANSWERS

1. What are the two tasks that the INDEX function can perform?

It can either return a single value in a specified position in a table or it can return a range of values in a specified location.

2. What is the following formula supposed to do: =INDEX(A2:E7,3,4)

Return the value in the third row of the fourth column of the data composed of Cells A2 through E7.

3. Does the INDEX function require you to include a header row or row labels in the specified cell range?

No. It's just returning a value in a specific location in a defined range.

4. How do you determine the row number value to use in the INDEX function?

It should be the number that corresponds to the order of the row within the defined range. It is not the actual row number in the Excel worksheet.

5. How do you determine the column number value to use in the INDEX function?

It should be the number that corresponds to the order of the column within the defined range. It is not the actual column number in the Excel worksheet.

6. Can you use the INDEX function with more than one table of data? How?

Yes. There is an optional fourth variable that can be included in the INDEX function that specifies which data table to pull the value from. In order to use it you have to provide multiple table ranges in the first input.

7. What happens if you use the fourth variable in the INDEX function without providing multiple table range values in the first variable?

You will get a #REF! error message.

8. If you want to use the INDEX function to pull an entire column or row of data, what do you need to do?

Use the function as an array formula. This means you highlight the cells where you want that data to go first, enter the formula in the first cell of that highlighted range, and then use Ctrl+Shift+Enter instead of Enter when you're done. To pull an entire column leave the row variable blank or set it to zero. To pull an entire row leave the column variable blank or set it to zero. For example, =INDEX(A2:E7,2,) and =INDEX(A2:E7,,3), will pull the entire second row and entire third column, respectively.

9. Can you easily copy and paste an array formula?

No.

10. Once you've extracted values from a table using the INDEX function are the results fixed values?

No. This is still a formula, so it's still pulling those values from the source table and any changes to the source table will change the values you pulled. The only way to fix the values is to then take the results and Copy and Paste Special-Values to remove the formula but keep the values.

THE MATCH FUNCTION QUIZ ANSWERS

1. What does the MATCH function do?

It returns the relative position of an item in a specified range of cells. It can also return the relative position of the closest value if there is no exact match in the range of cells as long as the values in the cells are properly sorted.

2. If the MATCH function returns a value of 2 for the following formula, what does that mean:
=MATCH($A12,$A$2:$A$7,0)

That an exact match to the value in Cell A12 is in the second row of the data in the range from Cell A2 through Cell A7. The first value is the value you're looking for, the second is the range of cells where that value may be, and the third value says that it should be an exact match.

3. What is the value in using the MATCH function?

It can be combined with other functions, like the INDEX function to facilitate looking up values in data tables.

4. What kinds of values can MATCH look for?

Numeric, text values, or logical values.

5. What are the three match types that you can use with MATCH?

You can look for an exact match, the smallest value that is greater than or equal to the specified value, or the largest value that is less than or equal to the specified value.

6. If you're not looking for an exact match what do you need to do first? And how will your choice of match type impact this?

You need to sort your data. If you're looking for the smallest value that is greater than the specified value sort in descending order. If you're looking for the largest value that is less than the specified value sort in ascending order.

7. What is the default match type used by MATCH? Why is this a problem?

If you don't specify a match type (-1,0,1) then Excel will assume you wanted to use the 1 match type and will look for the largest value that is less than or equal to the specified value. This is a problem if you haven't sorted your data to accommodate that type of match.

8. Is the value returned by MATCH the row number or the column number in the worksheet or something else?

It is not the row or column number in the worksheet. It is the relative row number or relative column number within the specified cell range.

TEXT FUNCTIONS QUIZ ANSWERS

1. What does the LEN function do?

It returns the number of characters in a text string.

2. What does the SEARCH function do?

It returns the number of the character at which a specific character or text string can first be found, reading from left to right.

3. What does the FIND function do?

It returns the starting position of one text string within another text string.

4. So what is the difference between SEARCH and FIND?

FIND is case-sensitive, so will treat "This" and "this" differently. It also does not allow the use of wildcards where SEARCH does allow them.

5. If you're working in a language such as Japanese, Chinese, or Korean that uses bytes instead of characters what functions should you use instead of LEN, SEARCH, and FIND?

LENB, SEARCHB, and FINDB.

6. What does the EXACT function do?

It returns a value of TRUE or FALSE based upon whether two text strings are exactly the same or not.

7. Is EXACT case-sensitive?

Yes. It will return a value of FALSE if used on "This" and "this", for example.

8. What result would LEN return for =LEN("This one")? Why?

8. Because it includes the space between "this" and "one" in the count of length.

9. Can you use LEN with a cell reference, so for example, =LEN(D10)?

Yes.

10. How does LEN handle a formula in a cell?

It returns a count of the length of the result of the formula. So if the formula returned a value of 8, then LEN would return a value of 1 in reference to that cell.

11. What is the following formula doing: =LEFT(A1,LEN(A1)-LEN(" units"))?

It's taking the left n-most characters from Cell A1 where n is equal to the total number of characters in Cell A1 minus the number of characters in " units". This is a way to extract the numeric value from an entry such as 12,000 units or 500 units where the number of characters in the numeric portion of the value is an unknown.

12. How could you accomplish the same task using the SEARCH function? Explain why this works.

=LEFT(A1,SEARCH(" units",A1)-1)

In this formula SEARCH returns the point at which

" units" can be found in the text contained in Cell A1. But we don't want that value because that would include the space in the result. So we take that value and subtract one from it to get just the number of units.

13. Do you have to start at the beginning of a text string if using the SEARCH or FIND functions?

No. You can use the optional third input to specify where in the text string to start the search.

14. If you do use the third input in the SEARCH or FIND function, what do you need to keep in mind about the value that's returned?

That even though you started at a point somewhere within the text string the numeric value returned is still going to be based upon the entire length of the text string. So if you used a 5 for that last value and the result was 7 that means it was only two characters past the fifth character in the string and seven from the beginning of the text string.

15. What will your result be if the value you search for using SEARCH or FIND isn't in that text string?

#VALUE!

16. What will your result be if the start position you provide is a negative number or a larger number than the length of the text string in SEARCH or FIND?

#VALUE!

17. What values will =SEARCH("coz*","teacozy") and =FIND("coz*","teacozy") return? Why?

SEARCH will return a value of 4. FIND will return a value of #VALUE!. That's because FIND does not work with wildcard characters like the * or the ?.

18. What values will =SEARCH("t","Teapot") and =FIND("t","Teapot") return? Why?

SEARCH will return a value of 1. FIND will return a value of 6. This is because FIND is case-sensitive, but SEARCH is not.

19. Does EXACT look for differences in formatting between two entries?

No.

20. If you wanted to compare the values in Cells A1 and D2, how would you write that using the EXACT function? What value would you expect if the two values were equal? What would you expect if they were not?

=EXACT(A1,D2)

TRUE. FALSE.

21. If you use EXACT with two cells that use different formulas but return the same numeric value, what will the result be?

TRUE. The EXACT function looks at the values returned by the two formulas and compares them to see if they're equal.

THE CONVERT FUNCTION QUIZ ANSWERS

1. What does the CONVERT function do?

It converts a number from one measurement system to another.

2. Name three types of conversions CONVERT can do:

Answers can include: Temperatures, distances, weights, units of time, units of energy, fluid measurements, speeds, etc.

3. What happens if you use units from two different categories in the same CONVERT function?

You'll receive an #N/A! error result.

4. Are the units used in the CONVERT function case-sensitive?

Yes. For example, "day" is a valid unit entry, but "Day" is not.

5. Write the formula for converting 57 degrees Fahrenheit to Celsius:

=CONVERT(57,"F","C")

6. Write the formula for determining how many days there are in five years using the CONVERT function:

=CONVERT(5,"yr","day")

7. Give a likely explanation for why the value returned in the last example is a decimal:

Because of leap years. There is one leap year every fourth year, so the calculation involves one-quarter of a day extra per year to account for that.

8. Write the formula for converting 60 miles to kilometers:

=CONVERT(60,"mi","km")

NUMERIC FUNCTIONS QUIZ
ANSWERS

1. What function would you use to take the absolute value of a number?

ABS

2. Write the function for the absolute value of -3:

=ABS(-3)

3. What does the MOD function do?

It takes one number divided by another and returns just the remainder.

4. What does the QUOTIENT function do?

It takes one number divided by another and returns just the integer portion of the resulting value.

5. Can you use the MOD and QUOTIENT functions to take a decimal number, such as 12.345 and separate the integer portion from the decimal portion? If so, how?

Yes. Assume the number is in Cell D3, you could use =MOD(D3,1) to extract the decimal portion and =QUOTIENT(D3,1) to extract the integer portion. This works because the division you're doing first keeps the number you started with.

6. What is another function that allows you to extract just the integer portion of a number?

The TRUNC function.

7. Apply this function to 12.345 to get 12:

=TRUNC(12.345,0) or =TRUNC(12.345)

8. What is the difference between truncating a number and rounding a number?

Truncating a number simply cuts the number off at that specific point. Rounding a number will take it to the next closest value based on rounding rules. So, for example, take the number 12.75 truncated or rounded. Truncating it will return a value of 12. Rounding it will return a value of 13.

9. How would you truncate 12,543 to the nearest 1000s?

=TRUNC(12543,-3)

10. Is this the same value you'd get if you rounded to the nearest 1000s?

No. That value, found using =ROUND(12543,-3) is 13000.

11. How does the INT function differ from the ROUND and TRUNC functions?

Like the ROUND and TRUNC functions, the INT function can also return the nearest integer value. ROUND and TRUNC can do more than this since you can specify at which point to round or truncate and INT is limited to just returning the nearest integer. Also, INT always rounds down to the nearest integer as opposed to TRUNC which simply chops off the decimal portion of a number and ROUND which will round up or down depending on which number is the closest. For positive values, INT and TRUNC return the same value but for negative values they never will.

12. How would you use the TRUNC function (and perhaps another function) to separate the number -12.345 into its integer and decimal components?

=TRUNC(-12.345) to get the integer and =ABS(-12.345-TRUNC(-12.345)) to get the decimal portion.

POWERS AND SQUARE ROOTS QUIZ ANSWERS

1. What does it mean to raise a number to a power?

It means that you multiply a number by itself that specified number of times. So 3 raised to the power of 2 means that you multiply 3 times 3.

2. What function can be used to do this?

The POWER function.

3. Is there a way to do this with notation instead? How?

Yes. The carat ^ will do the same thing.

4. Show how to take 5 to the power of 4 using both the function and the notation method.

=POWER(5,4)

=5^4

5. Can you use both of these methods to take a root power, such as the square root of a number? If so, write how to take the square root of 9.

=POWER(9,.5)
=9^.5

6. Is there a function that will specifically let you take the square root of a number? What is it? Apply it to 9.
Yes. SQRT. =SQRT(9)

7. What is the function that will let you return the value of Pi to fifteen digits?
PI

8. How would you write that?
=PI()

9. How would you calculate the area of a circle (which is Pi times the square of the radius) using the above functions where the radius is 3?
=PI()*(3^2)
=PI()*POWER(3,2)

10. What does the function SQRTPI give you?
The square root of a number times Pi.

11. If you wanted the square root of Pi itself, how could you get that value?
=PI()^.5
=SQRTPI(1)

LOGARITHMS QUIZ ANSWERS

1. What formula would you use to obtain the value of *e*?

=EXP(1)

2. What does the function used in the prior question do?

It returns the value *e* raised to the given power where *e* is an irrational and transcendental number with an approximate value of 2.718.

3. What is =LOG(100) asking?

It's asking what power you'd have to take the number 10 to in order to get a value of 100. In this case, the answer is 2.

4. Write a formula that uses the LOG function to determine what power you'd have to take the number 2 to get a result of 24:

=LOG(24,2)

5. Write a formula that uses the LOG function to determine what power you'd have to take *e* to to get a

result of 24:
    =LOG(24,EXP(1))

6. Write a formula that uses the LN function to make the same determination:
    =LN(24)

7. What does the LN function do?
It takes the natural logarithm of a number.

8. What does the LOG function do?
It returns the logarithm of a number to the base you specify.

9. Which of the two is more flexible?
The LOG function because it can perform the calculation the LN function does as well as use other bases.

10. What does the LOG10 function do?
It returns the base ten logarithm of a number.

11. Should you use it?
No need to because LOG will by default do the same thing.

FACTORIALS AND COMBINATIONS QUIZ ANSWERS

1. What is the difference between permutations and combinations?

Permutations are ordered combinations. So with a permutations 123 and 321 are not the same. But with a combination they are because they both contain the same three values: 1, 2, and 3. If you were dividing ten people into teams of two, you'd want to use combinations because it doesn't matter if Gary is assigned to a group first or Bob is, at the end of the day you have a group that contains Gary and Bob. But if you were rank-ordering those same ten people then it does matter who is assigned first place, second place, etc. so you'd want to use permutations.

2. What does a factorial do?

It calculates the number of unique permutations you can generate given a specified sample size. So there are six permutations when you have three choices: 123, 132, 231, 213, 312, and 321.

3. What function in Excel will do this calculation for you?

FACT

4. What formula would you write to determine the number of possible permutations for a group of ten people?

=FACT(10)

5. What happens with the FACT function if you input a decimal value, for example =FACT(3.95)?

It will truncate the number provided and then do the factorial calculation. So in this case it would return the equivalent of =FACT(3).

6. What value will Excel return if you ask for the factorial of zero?

One.

7. What happens if you ask for the factorial of a negative number?

You'll get a #NUM! error message.

8. If you had a group of ten individuals and wanted to give out first, second, and third place medals, how would you use the FACT function to calculate the number of possible three-person outcomes?

=FACT(10)/FACT(10-3)

9. What if you instead wanted to calculate the number of three-person teams that could be built out of a population of nine people. What function would you use?

COMBIN

10. What does this function do?

It calculates the number of combinations for a given number of items.

11. How would you use it to calculate the number of two-person teams possible in a group of four individuals?

=COMBIN(4,2)

You can work this out on paper as well to check it. Your teams are 12, 13, 14, 23, 24, and 34.

12. What function would you use if you want to know the number of possible combinations where each possibility can be chosen multiple times? (In other words, you can have 22 as an outcome.)

COMBINA

13. So if you had a raffle drawing and there were ten people participating, each with one ticket and where each ticket was put back into the draw each time, and you wanted to know the odds of one person winning all three draws how would you do that calculation?

First calculate the total number of possible unique outcomes by using =COMBINA(10,3).

Then divide one (that's how many times one person would win all three draws) by the total number of possible outcomes to get the percentage of times that one person would've been expected to win all three raffles.

PRESENT AND FUTURE VALUES QUIZ ANSWERS

1. If you want to know the current value of a series of identical payments that you'll receive on an annual basis in the future, what function can you use to calculate that?

PV

2. What are the inputs to this function?

Rate: This is the rate you'll be paid (or pay) per period

Nper: This is the number of payment periods

Pmt: This is the amount you will receive or pay for each period

Fv: Is a lump sum payment that you'll receive or pay out at the very end of all payment periods

Type: Dictates when payments are made, either at the beginning of the payment period or at the end of the payment period. By default the assumption is that payments will be made at the end of the period.

3. What does the NPV function do?

Returns the net present value of an investment based

on a discount rate and a series of future cash flows (either incoming or outgoing).

4. What is the advantage of the NPV function over the PV function?

With the NPV function your payments can be different amounts whereas the PV function requires that the periodic payments be the same amount each period.

5. What limitation do both PV and NPV share?

The time period between each inflow or outflow must be the same.

6. If I have a range of values in Cells B2 through B8 that represent annual payments that I'm going to receive starting one year from now and want to calculate the net present value of those amounts using a ten percent annual interest rate, how would I write that:

=NPV(.1,B2:B8)

7. What if I'm going to receive $1,000 each year for the next five years and the annual interest rate is 10%. What formula would you write to calculate the current value of those future payments?

=PV(.1,5,1000)

You could also write a formula using NPV, such as =NPV(0.1,B2:B6), and get the same result.

8. What does the FORECAST function do?

It calculates a value for y given a specified value for x and existing known values for x and y. Predictions are made assuming a linear trend.

9. Why is it important to remember that it only works with a linear trend?

Because many relationships that occur in life are not in

fact linear and so the forecasted value will not necessarily be accurate.

10. Because of this, what should you do before using the FORECAST function?

Plot your data to see if it's following a linear or near linear trend. If it isn't, don't use FORECAST. Note that there is another forecasting function available starting with Excel 2016 that you can use instead in those instances.

11. What are the order of the inputs to the FORECAST function?

You list the x you want Excel to use in its prediction, then a range for all of the known y values, and then a corresponding range for all of the known x values.

12. Can you use FORECAST to predict a value prior to your data range? In other words, what y would be at a smaller value of x than is shown in your data table?

Yes. Just be careful if you've converted any time range (such as months) to a number for purposes of using the function because it will consider the 0 point as a point within the range.

THE FREQUENCY FUNCTION QUIZ ANSWERS

1. What does the FREQUENCY function do?

It takes a list of values and calculates how many occurrences of those values fall within ranges specified by the user.

2. What must you have in order to use the FREQUENCY function?

A series of "bin" values for the function to use so that it knows how to define each range.

3. What does it mean that FREQUENCY is an array function?

That it will return more than one value. This means that you have to highlight the cells where you want your answers returned first, then you type the formula in the first cell of the range, and then you use Ctrl+Shift+Enter to finish the calculation.

4. What are the inputs to the FREQUENCY function?

Data Array: This is the range of cells that include the data whose frequency you want to calculate.

Bins Array: This is the range of cells that define the bins you want to use for the calculation.

5. How is a bins array entry structured? And how is it used by Excel?

Each bin in the array is a single numeric value entered in a cell. For the first cell in a bins array, Excel will calculate the number of cells in the data array that have a value less than or equal to that value. For the next cell it will calculate the number of cells that have a value greater than the last one but less than or equal to the current cell. And so on. The final bins array, if it's blank will be used to calculate any entries greater than the last specified value.

6. What is an easy way to get a list of bin array values that correspond to all potential values in your data set?

Copy and paste those values into a new range and then use the Remove Duplicates option under Data Tools in the Data tab to get a list of unique values from the original range.

7. If the range of values you want to evaluate are in Column C and your bins values are in Cells D2 through D6, how would you write the formula to calculate your frequencies for each of those bin values?

=FREQUENCY(C:C,D2:D6)

THE HOW EXCEL HANDLES DATES QUIZ ANSWERS

1. By default what does the number 1 represent with respect to a date in Excel?

The date January 1, 1900. It can also represent the value for a single day.

2. Can Excel handle dates prior to 1900?

No.

3. Can you use addition and subtraction with dates in Excel? Why or why not?

Yes. Because each date in Excel is treated like a number, you can use addition and subtraction with dates in Excel.

4. What is a serial_number with respect to date functions in Excel?

The numeric value for a date. In many functions this can also just be a reference to the date itself.

5. How does Excel handle dates differently on the Mac operating system? What does this mean for someone working between a PC and a Mac using Excel?

On Macs the beginning date is not January 1, 1900 but is instead January 2, 1904. That means there is a difference of 1,462 days between the value assigned to a specific date in Excel on a PC and that same date on a Mac.

6. How does Excel account for this?

Excel is set up to store dates according to one or the other system and that is specified in the File Options.

7. If you enter a two-digit year, for example '29, how will Excel treat that in terms of the century it applies?

For two-digit years between 00 and 29 it will interpret that as a date set in the 2000s, so 2000 to 2029. For two-digit years between 30 and 99 it will treat that as a date set in the 1900s, so 1930 to 1999.

DATE FUNCTIONS
QUIZ ANSWERS

1. What does the DATE function do?

It takes a specified year, month, and day of the month and returns a date. So =DATE(1900,1,1) will return a value of 1/1/1900. (Or whatever format you're using for your dates. If no date format automatically applies to a cell it will return the numeric value, in this case 1.)

2. What happens if you use the DATE function with a date prior to January 1, 1900, so for example if you use =DATE(1880,1,1)?

Excel will add the year value you provided to 1900 to provide the date. So =DATE(1880,1,1) becomes 1/1/3780.

3. Can you use a value for the month portion of the DATE function that is greater than 12? What about less than 1?

Yes. If you do so, Excel will take the year and day of the month provided and add that many months. If the number for months provided is negative it will subtract that many months, but it includes a value of zero as a legitimate month count. So =DATE(1905,-2,1) will go back to October 1, 1904 which is January minus three months.

4. What about days of the month? Can you have a number greater than 31 or a negative number?

Yes. It works the same way as the months do. It will carry forward that many days or if it goes backward it will go back that many days plus one additional day.

5. Write a formula that takes a date stored in Cell B2 and adds four months to it.

=DATE(YEAR(B2),MONTH(B2)+4,DAY(B2))

6. What does the YEAR function do?

It returns the year portion of a date in the integer range of 1900 through 9999.

7. How would you use YEAR to extract the year portion of the date March 1, 2010?

=YEAR("March, 1, 2010")
=YEAR("3/1/2010")
=YEAR("3-1-2010")
=YEAR(A1) where A1 contains the date

8. What happens if you fail to use quotation marks around a date used in a YEAR function?

You will get a #NUM! error message.

9. What does the MONTH function do?

It returns the month portion of a date in numeric form where January is represented by the number 1 and December is represented by the number 12.

10. What result will you get from =MONTH("April, 1, 1952")?

4

11. What does the DAY function do?

It returns the day portion of a date in numeric form from 1 to 31.

12. What does the HOUR function do?

It returns the hour component of a date/time in numeric form from 0 (which represents midnight) to 23 (which represents eleven o'clock in the evening).

13. What will =HOUR(NOW()) give you?

The current hour. For me it's currently five o'clock at night, so that value would be 17.

14. Since Excel treats dates as numbers, what is the value of an hour under Excel's system?

.041667 which is the equivalent of 1/24

15. Will you get a result with =HOUR(.166667)?

Yes. It will return a value of 4.

16. How does the MINUTE function work?

It returns the minute portion of a date/time in numeric form from 0 to 59.

17. Since Excel treats dates as numbers, what is the value of a minute under Excel's system?

.000694 or 1/60 of 1/24

18. What does the SECOND function do?

Returns the second portion of a date/time in the range from 0 to 59.

**19. What result will you get from
=SECOND("12:32:21")?**

21

20. Since Excel treats dates as numbers, what is the value of a second under Excel's system?

.000011574 or 1/60 of 1/60 of 1/24

21. If you enter a date without entering a specific time of day and then use the HOUR, MINUTE, or SECOND function on that date, what value will Excel give you?

0

22. What does the WEEKDAY function do?

It returns the day of the week for a specified date using a value of 1 through 7 where the day of the week represented by each number is dependent upon the setting specified by the user.

23. What is the default setting for the WEEKDAY function in terms of numbering the days of the week?

By default, 1 will equal Sunday and so on until 7 equals Saturday.

24. If August 13, 2019 is a Tuesday and I use =WEEKDAY("August 13, 2019") what value will I get back?

3

25. What portion of the WEEKDAY function should you change if you want the numbers returned to map to different days of the week? How would you change the above formula so that Monday is treated as a 1 and Tuesday returns a value of 2 instead?

The optional return_type variable lets you specify which day of the week is considered the first day of the week. To change =WEEKDAY("August 13, 2019") so that Monday is the first day of the week and any Tuesday is a value of 2 you would write =WEEKDAY("August 13, 2019",2) or =WEEKDAY("August 13, 2019",11)

26. What does the following formula do:
=IF(WEEKDAY(A1,2)>5,12.95,9.95)

It says that if the date in Cell A1 using a numbering standard where Monday is 1 through to Sunday is 7 is greater than 5 (so a Saturday or Sunday) then return a value of 12.95. If it is 5 or less (so Monday through Friday) then return a value of 9.95.

27. What does the WEEKNUM function do?

It returns a number for which week in the year a date is part of. However, it returns values up to 53.

28. How does Excel define a week for purposes of the WEEKNUM function?

That depends on the return_type you choose. The default is for Excel to define a week as starting on a Sunday and to only include dates for that given year. So, for example, for 2019 week 1 was January 1st, a Tuesday, through January 5th, a Saturday. This can be adjusted so that any day of the week is considered the start point.

29. How do you get Excel to define a week in accordance with ISO standards when using the WEEKNUM function? And how does it work?

By setting the return_type value to 21. Excel takes the first week of the year that has a Thursday in it and starts the week on the Monday of that week even if the Monday of that week falls in the prior year.

30. What is another function you can use to get Excel to apply the ISO standard when determining the week number? And when did it become available?

ISOWEEKNUM which became available in Excel 2013

DATE CALCULATION FUNCTIONS IN EXCEL QUIZ ANSWERS

1. What does the DAYS function do?

It takes a given start date and a given end date and calculates the difference between them in terms of the number of days.

2. Do you need the DAYS function to do this?

No. You can also just use simple subtraction and put the dates in quote marks. For example, ="12/25/18"-"6/1/18" or =B1-C1 where the dates are stored in those cells.

3. What does the DAYS360 function do?

The DAYS360 function calculates the number of days between two dates assuming that all months have thirty days in them. (This is useful in some financial calculations.)

4. Are there different methods with DAYS360 for handling the last day of the month when it's either in February or in a month with 31 days?

Yes. The default is the U.S. or NASD method but you can also set it to use the European method.

5. What does the EDATE function do?

The EDATE function returns the serial number of the date that is the indicated number of months before or after the specified start date.

6. What is another way to get this same result?

Use the DATE function to extract YEAR, MONTH, and DAY from a date and then add the desired number of months to the MONTH value.

7. If I use =EDATE("March 1, 2019",4) what result will that give me?

43647 which is equivalent to July 1, 2019 because it takes that date and moves the month portion only forward the specified number of months. If I were to take that date and add 120 days to it, four months times thirty days, I would get a different result.

8. How does EDATE handle partial month values, such as =EDATE("March 1, 2019",4.9)?

It truncates the provided value, so this would be the equivalent of =EDATE("March 1, 2019",4)

9. What does the EOMONTH function do?

Returns the last day of the month before or after a specified number of months in serial number format.

10. What do you need to do with the result of an EDATE or EOMONTH formula?

Format it as a date because it will be a number until you do.

WORKDAYS AND NETWORKDAYS QUIZ ANSWERS

1. What does the NETWORKDAYS function do?

It allows you to calculate the number of whole workdays between two dates.

2. How is this different from just using the DAYS function?

The DAYS function treats all days as the same. The NETWORKDAYS function will not include weekend days. However, the NETWORKDAYS function does count the start date and end date provided in its calculation whereas the DAYS function doesn't include the start date.

3. How can you incorporate holidays into the NETWORKDAYS function?

By using the optional third input for holidays. You can either provide a list of the holidays within curvy brackets { } or you can put the dates into a table and reference their location as your third input.

4. What if you don't want NETWORKDAYS to include the start date and the end date in the calculation?

You can follow the NETWORKDAYS function portion with subtraction to take out either the start date only (-1) or both the start and end dates (-2) from the count.

5. Using NETWORKDAYS write a formula calculating the number of workdays between August 28, 2019 and September 4, 2019 where September 2, 2019 is a holiday and you don't want to count the first or the last day in the count:

=NETWORKDAYS("8/28/19","9/4/19","9/2/19")-2

The answer is 3. There are a few other ways to write it, but this is one example.

6. What function would you use to calculate workdays if your weekend days are not Saturday and Sunday?

NETWORKDAYS.INTL

7. With which version of Excel did this function become available?

Excel 2010

8. Explain what the weekend input to the NETWORKDAYS.INTL function does:

It allows you to specify a custom weekend parameter. You can have a "weekend" that is only one day of the week or a weekend that consists of any two continuous days within the week by using this input. The values are listed in a dropdown menu.

9. Are NETWORKDAYS and NETWORKDAYS.INTL directly interchangeable? Can you just change one to the other and have it work?

No. Not if you used the holidays input for either function or the weekend input for the NETWORKDAYS.INTL function, because the third input for NETWORKDAYS is the list of holidays but that's the fourth input in the NETWORKDAYS.INTL function.

10. What does the WORKDAY function do?

It returns the value for the date that is before or after a specified number of workdays.

11. Does WORKDAY include the start date in its count like NETWORKDAYS does?

No.

12. What does the WORKDAY.INTL function do?

It returns the value for the date that is before or after a specified number of workdays but also allows for custom weekend parameters.

13. Let's say that your team is working six-day weeks and that they're allowed to have Wednesdays off. It's currently August 23, 2019 and your team says they need twelve more days to finish the project. There is a holiday on September 2, 2019. When will they complete the project?

September 7, 2019
=WORKDAY.INTL("August 23, 2019",12,14,
"September 2, 2019")

14. What if they tell you this on the morning of the 23rd and you know that they'll be working all day so it will count towards their timeline. Will this impact the completion date?

Yes. Because WORKDAY and WORKDAY.INTL do not count the current date in their calculations.

September 6, 2019

=WORKDAY.INTL("August 23, 2019",11,14,
"September 2, 2019")

15. Can you create a custom set of off days using the WORKDAY.INTL function? How?

Yes. By inputting a binary string of values that shows which days are "on" and which days are "off" days where off days are shown using a 1 and on days are shown using a 0.

COMBINING FUNCTIONS
QUIZ ANSWERS

1. Is it possible to write a formula that uses more than one function?

Absolutely.

2. How would you write a formula that returns a value of TRUE if the value in Cell A1 is greater than 10 or the value in Cell B1 is greater than 10 and a value of FALSE otherwise?

=IF(OR(A1>10,B1>10),TRUE(),FALSE())

Note that that used four different functions in one formula.

3. What do you need to be careful about when combining functions together in one formula?

That you have all of your parens in the right place and don't forget any.

4. Do you need to use an equals sign in front of each function name when you combine functions in a single formula?

No. You just need to start your formula with an equals sign, but that's it.

5. What should you explore further if you're running into file size issues because of repeat calculations in your Excel worksheet?

Array formulas.

WHEN THINGS GO WRONG
QUIZ ANSWERS

1. Name five different error messages you might see.

#REF!, #VALUE!, #DIV/0!, #N/A, #NUM!

You also might see a comment that you've created a circular references or have too few arguments or that the formula you've written doesn't work and Excel wants to fix it for you.

2. What does #REF! generally indicate?

That you've deleted a value that was being referenced in that cell. For example, =A1+B1 will generate that message if you delete Column A or Column B.

3. How can you see where the cell that was deleted was located in your formula?

Click on the cell and look in the formula bar or double-click on the cell. The cell reference that's missing will have been replaced with #REF!.

4. What does a #VALUE! message indicate?

That the cell you're referencing is the wrong type of cell for that function. So maybe you have a date or number formatted as plain text, for example. In rare cases it could also mean that you have regional settings that impact how you're supposed to write your functions. It can also mean that you're referencing a now unavailable outside data source.

5. What does a #DIV/0! message indicate?

That you're dividing by zero or a blank cell.

6. If the #DIV/0! message is legitimate because nothing has been entered yet, what's a quick way to suppress it?

Use an IF function in that cell rather than just a division formula. So instead of having =A1/B1, have =IF(B1<>0,A1/B1,"").

7. What does a #N/A error message generally mean?

That Excel isn't finding what it was asked to look for.

8. What can you check for if this happens and you don't think it should have?

Check the formatting of your values to make sure they match. Also check that there aren't extra spaces in one of your inputs or lookup values.

9. What does the IFERROR function do? What do you need to be careful with if you use it?

Suppresses an error result and replaces it with a zero, a blank space, or text that you provide. It will suppress all error messages, even ones you may want to see.

10. What does the #NUM! error message generally indicate?

That there are numeric values in a function that are not valid. It also happens when the function is going to return a result that is too large or too small or can't find a solution.

11. What is a circular reference?

One that references itself. So if in Cell A1 I write =A1+B1 that is circular because to generate the answer in Cell A1 I would have to use the value in Cell A1. That would create a continuous loop if you actually tried to do it.

12. If you don't think you have a circular reference but Excel tells you you do, what should you check for?

That you haven't created an indirect circular reference. For example, if you write in Cell A1 =B1+C1 that looks fine. But if the value in C1 is calculated by =SUM(A:A) then you're using the value in Cell A1 to calculate the value in Cell C1 and can't also use it to calculate the value in Cell A1.

13. If you're trying to figure out what cells are feeding the value in a cell where can you go to do that?

Trace Precedents under Formula Auditing in the Formulas tab.

14. If Excel tells you you have too few arguments, what should you check for?

First, that you've included all required inputs for that particular function. In the function description anything listed with brackets is optional, but anything listed as text without brackets is not. Also, check that you have all of your parens and commas and quotation marks in the right places.

15. What can you do with a formula that just isn't working the way it should be?

Double-click on the formula and check that all of the cell references are pointing to the right cells. Also, if you're copying a formula make sure that you used $ signs to lock any cell references that need to be locked. Also make sure that any options for that function were chosen properly. (Exact versus approximate, ascending vs. descending, etc.)

(And one that isn't in the guide, but came up as I was writing this, if you copied from Word into Excel make sure that you replace any curly quotes or smart quotes with straight quotes. Excel will not accept smart quotes.)

CELL NOTATION
QUIZ ANSWERS

1. What is Cell A1 referencing?
The cell that's in Column A and Row 1.

2. Name two ways you can reference more than one cell in a function.
With a comma between individual cells, row references, or column references. Or with a colon to reference a range of cells, rows, or columns.

For example:
=SUM(A1, B1, C1)
or
=SUM(A:A,B:B,C:C)
or
=SUM(1:1,2:2,3:3)
or
=SUM(A1:C1)
or
=SUM(A:C)
or
=SUM(1:3)

3. Can you reference a cell in another worksheet?

Yes. You just need to include the worksheet name reference as well.

4. Can you reference a cell in another workbook?

Yes. You just need to include the workbook name reference as well, but be careful doing so because the formula may not work if that other workbook is moved, renamed, or deleted.

5. What's an easy way to reference a cell in another worksheet or workbook?

Start your formula and then just click on the cell you need. Excel will write the cell reference for you.

BONUS: EXERCISES

EXERCISE 1

You have a project that you are managing. The start date of the project is July 1, 2019 and will need to be finished by August 30, 2019. Assume the only holiday is July 4, 2019.

1. Assuming a standard U.S. workweek with Saturdays and Sundays off, how many days will this give you to complete the project?

2. The team lead for the first leg of the project says that she needs fifteen working days to complete her portion. What day should you expect her to be completed by assuming her team will begin work on July 1st.

3. Assume that you have ten people assigned to this project and that you want to put them into two teams of five. How many possible team configurations do you have to choose from?

4. The project requires completing 500 widgets during the project period. Assuming that in the first three weeks you produce 68, 84, and 72 widgets, respectively, and

that this phase of the project has six weeks for completion, and that there will be no significant changes to the production rate, will you reach your goal? If not, approximately how many widgets will you have produced by the end of the six-week period?

EXERCISE 2

Take the following table of units sold by each of three sales people for each of three products.

	A	B	C	D
		Jane	Javier	Mo
1		Jane	Javier	Mo
2	Widgets	25	22	24
3	Whatchamacallits	15	18	30
4	Thingies	12	20	15

1. Build a table that lists the salesperson name in rows and the product name in each column and remains linked to the original table of data.

2. Write a formula that will look in the original table for the number of Whatchamacallits sold by Javier using a search for Javier's name.

3. Write a formula that will look in the original table for the number of Whatchamacallits sold by Javier assuming that you won't know which column Javier is

in nor will you know which column Whatchamacallits are in.

EXERCISE 3

1. Take the following value in Cell A1, $121/hr, and write a formula that will extract the dollar portion of the entry only.

2. Write a formula to calculate at what point in the above entry the / starts?

3. You have a cube that is 2 foot by 2 foot by 2 foot. Write a formula to calculate the area of that cube in feet using exponents. Write a formula to calculate the area of the cube in meters.

EXERCISE 4

1. Write a formula to calculate how often each of the following values occurs: 2, 2, 2, 6, 6, 6, 6, 8, 8, 9, 9, 9, 9

EXERCISE 5

1. Assume that you're thinking of buying a car. Your options are to pay $5,500 now or to pay monthly payments of $125 per month for the next four years. Assuming that the relative interest rate is 5%, which should you choose to do?

2. Which is better: To pay $5,000 now or to pay $5,250 in five years assuming there's a 10% rate per year?

3. What amount would you have to invest today to generate $5,250 in five years assuming a 10% rate per year?

4. How does that combine with your answer to the question before it?

BONUS:
EXERCISE ANSWERS

EXERCISE 1

You have a project that you are managing. The start date of the project is July 1, 2019 and will need to be finished by August 30, 2019. Assume the only holiday is July 4, 2019.

1. **Assuming a standard U.S. workweek with Saturdays and Sundays off, how many days will this give you to complete the project?**

   44
   =NETWORKDAYS("July 1, 2019","August 30, 2019","July 4, 2019")

2. **The team lead for the first leg of the project says that she needs fifteen working days to complete her portion. What day should you expect her to be completed by assuming her team will begin work on July 1st.**

   July 22, 2019
   =WORKDAY("July 1, 2019",15-1,"July 4, 2019")

3. **Assume that you have ten people assigned to this project and that you want to put them into two teams of five. How many possible team configurations do you have to choose from?**

    252

    =COMBIN(10,5)

4. **The project requires completing 500 widgets during the project period. Assuming that in the first three weeks you produce 68, 84, and 72 widgets, respectively, and that this phase of the project has six weeks for completion, and that there will be no significant changes to the production rate, will you reach your goal? If not, approximately how many widgets will you have produced by the end of the six-week period?**

    No. Approximately 466 widgets will be produced. This can be calculated using the FORECAST function to predict output for weeks four, five, and six.

    For the first three weeks we have 224 widgets. If you then put those into a table, say in Cells A1 through B4 where Column A has the week number and Column B has the number of widgets made in that week, you can then use FORECAST to predict the number of widgets produced in weeks 4, 5, and 6, respectively.

    =FORECAST(4,$B$2:$B$4,$A$2:$A$4)

    =FORECAST(5,$B$2:$B$4,$A$2:$A$4)

    =FORECAST(6,$B$2:$B$4,$A$2:$A$4)

    The values predicted are 78.67, 80.67, and 82.67 which when added to the 224 from the first three weeks is approximately 466 widgets.

	A	B	C
1	Week	Widgets	
2	1	68	
3	2	84	
4	3	72	
5			
6			FORECAST
7	Week	Widgets	Formula
8	4	78.66667	=FORECAST(4,$B$2:$B$4,$A$2:$A$4)
9	5	80.66667	=FORECAST(5,$B$2:$B$4,$A$2:$A$4)
10	6	82.66667	=FORECAST(6,$B$2:$B$4,$A$2:$A$4)

EXERCISE 2

Take the following table of units sold by each of three sales people for each of three products.

	A	B	C	D
1		Jane	Javier	Mo
2	Widgets	25	22	24
3	Whatchamacallits	15	18	30
4	Thingies	12	20	15

1. **Build a table that lists the salesperson name in rows and the product name in each column and remains linked to the original table of data.**

    This can be done easily with the TRANSPOSE function. Highlight an area that is four cells by four cells, type =TRANSPOSE(A1:D4) in the first cell while the others remain highlighted, and then use Ctrl+Shift+Enter to populate the four cells. To remove the 0 value in the top left corner of the table you can go to the corresponding cell in the original table and type ="" into that cell and then hit Enter.

2. **Write a formula that will look in the original table for the number of Whatchamacallits sold by Javier using a search for Javier's name.**

   =HLOOKUP("Javier",A1:D4,3)

3. **Write a formula that will look in the original table for the number of Whatchamacallits sold by Javier assuming that you won't know which column Javier is in nor will you know which column Whatchamacallits are in:**

   =INDEX(A1:D4,MATCH("Whatchamacallits",A1:A 4,0),MATCH("Javier",A1:D1,0))

EXERCISE 3

1. Take the following value in Cell A1, $121/hr, and write a formula that will extract the dollar portion of the entry only.

    =LEFT(A1,LEN(A1)-LEN("/hr"))

2. Write a formula to calculate at what point in the above entry the / starts?

    =SEARCH("/",A1)

3. You have a cube that is 2 foot by 2 foot by 2 foot. Write a formula to calculate the area of that cube in feet using exponents. Write a formula to calculate the area of the cube in meters.

    =2^3 or
    =POWER(2,3)

    =(CONVERT(2,"ft","m"))^3 or
    =CONVERT(POWER(2,3),"ft^3","m^3")

EXERCISE 4

1. **Write a formula to calculate how often each of the following values occurs: 2, 2, 2, 6, 6, 6, 6, 8, 8, 9, 9, 9, 9**

Put the values into one cell each to make a table. Copy those values to a new location and remove duplicates. (Or create your own table of the unique values.) Highlight the cells in the next column that are next to the unique values and use the FREQUENCY function to calculate occurrence of each one. This is an array function so be sure to use Ctrl+Shift+Enter instead of Enter.

	A	B	C	D
1	Entries		Value	Occurrence
2	2		2	3
3	2		6	4
4	2		8	2
5	6		9	4
6	6			
7	6			
8	6			
9	8			
10	8			
11	9			
12	9			
13	9			
14	9			

In this example, the formula was

=FREQUENCY(A2:A14,C2:C5)

since the original values were in Cells A2 through A14 and the unique values were in Cells C2 through C5.

EXERCISE 5

1. **Assume that you're thinking of buying a car. Your options are to pay $5,500 now or to pay monthly payments of $125 per month for the next four years. Assuming that the relative interest rate is 5%, which should you choose to do?**

You should take the payments.

Even though you pay $6,000 for the entire term of the loan (125*48), the present value of those payments is only $5,427 which is less than the $5,500 you would pay out of pocket. This is calculated using
$$=-PV((0.05/12),48,125)$$

2. **Which is better: To pay $5,000 now or to pay $5,250 in five years assuming there's a 10% rate per year?**

Pay $5,250 in five years. The net present value of $5,250 in five years at a 10% rate is only $3,105. This can be calculated using:
$$=NPV(0.1,0,0,0,0,5000) \text{ or } =5000/(1.1^5).$$

3. **What amount would you have to invest today to generate $5,250 in five years assuming a 10% rate per year?**

    $3,259.84

    You can calculate this using

    $$=NPV(0.1,0,0,0,0,5250)$$

4. **How does that combine with your answer to the question before it?**

    This means that you could take your $5,000 you have now, invest $3,260 worth of it at 10% to make that $5,250 payment in five years and spend the rest of it and still meet your obligation so it justifies choosing to pay the $5,250 in five years rather than $5,000 now.

INDEX OF QUIZZES

ABOUT THE AUTHOR

M.L. Humphrey is a former stockbroker with a degree in Economics from Stanford and an MBA from Wharton who has spent close to twenty years as a regulator and consultant in the financial services industry.

You can reach M.L. at mlhumphreywriter@gmail.com or at mlhumphrey.com.